> "I am not unmindful that some of ____ of great trials and tribulations.... You have been the veterans of creative suffering. Continue to work with the faith that unearned suffering is redemptive."

--- Dr. Martin Luther King, Jr. from his famous "I Have A Dream" speech (1963)

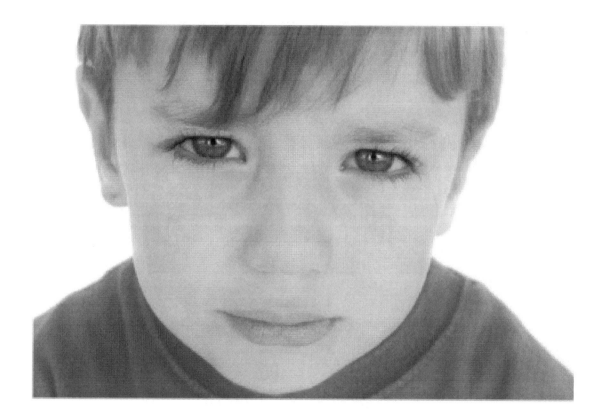

This workbook is dedicated to the children whose voices have not yet been heard.

Childhood means simplicity. Look at the world with the child's eye - it is very beautiful.

---- Kailash Satyarthi

Table of Contents

Let us remember: One book, one pen, one child, and one teacher can change the world.

-- Malala Yousafzai

Introduction

Helping the Traumatized Child is designed as a tool for therapists to use with children and adolescents who have experienced trauma. The activities in this workbook are based on cutting-edge research in the field of trauma treatment for children. Studies have found that educating children about trauma, providing positive stress management techniques, re-exposing the child to the traumatic events, and changing children's distorted thoughts about the trauma, are all effective strategies for ameliorating the symptoms of Post-Traumatic Stress Disorder (PTSD).[1] This book offers the therapist these sound scientific methods in an easy to use, child-friendly form. The activities are best used with children ages seven to eighteen, but can be tailored for children as young as four-years old.

This workbook is not designed to be used alone, but rather as a companion to an existing knowledge base of trauma treatment with children. Basic principles of child psychotherapy and child maltreatment are not included in this text. It is recommended, therefore, that, while using this manual, clinicians read other sources for treating traumatized children. I suggest the book Treating Trauma and Traumatic Grief in Children and Adolescents by Judith Cohen, PhD, Anthony Mannarino, PhD and Esther Deblinger, PhD. This text is a great starting point for learning how to treat traumatized children. I have also provided a resource for other books on trauma in Appendix B.

In addition to reading one or more of the recommended books, I suggest seeking out a training program in your area that can provide a deeper understanding of child maltreatment and trauma-specific child psychotherapy. Check with the National Child Traumatic Stress Network (www.nctsn.org) for more information on programs in your area. The Medical University of South Carolina, in partnership with the NCTSN, offers an excellent online training called Trauma-Focused Cognitive Behavioral Therapy.

This workbook follows the proven patterns of treatment considered effective by researchers with the National Child Traumatic Stress Network. Below is a basic overview of the chapter titles in this workbook and the corresponding goals of trauma treatment.

---

[1]   (Cohen, J. A., Mannarino, A. P., & Knudsen, K. , 2004)

Check out http://www.tfcbt.musc.edu for an excellent web-based learning program on trauma therapy for children and teenagers.

1. **"Getting to Know Me"**
   Goal: Assessment & Goal Setting

2. **"What is Trauma & Abuse?"**
   Goal: Psycho-education of Trauma and Abuse

3. **"Managing My Emotions"**
   Goal: Emotion Identification & Regulation

4. **"Managing Stress"**
   Goal: Relaxation Training & Thought Stopping

5. **"Managing My Thoughts"**
   Goal: Connecting Thoughts to Feelings and Actions

6. **"Trauma Timeline"**
   Goal: Outlining Traumatic Events

7. **"Trauma Narrative"**
   Goal: Exposure of Traumatic Events with Thoughts & Feelings

8. **"Changing Unhelpful Thoughts"**
   Goal: Reprocessing Distorted Thoughts

9. **"Being Safe"**
   Goal: Sharing Trauma Narrative w/Caregiver. Safety Planning & Graduation

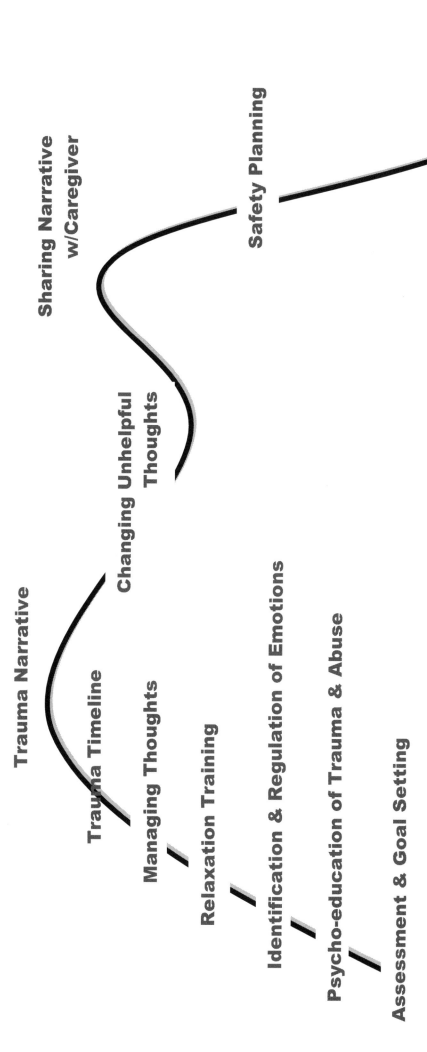

The Arc of Exposure

This graph shows the stages of treatment and the arc of exposure for the child to their traumatic event(s). It is important to note that exposure begins during the assessment phase and continues throughout treatment.

Trauma Narrative

Sharing Narrative w/Caregiver

Changing Unhelpful Thoughts

Trauma Timeline

Managing Thoughts

Relaxation Training

Safety Planning

Identification & Regulation of Emotions

Psycho-education of Trauma & Abuse

Assessment & Goal Setting

Graduation & Celebration

Making Therapy Fun

Trauma therapy does not have to be painful and arduous for the therapist or the child. While parts of treatment may be emotionally challenging for the child, it is still important to engage her to keep her focused on the tasks at hand. To this end, I have created a point system that can be implemented to motivate the child to complete the assignments, both in therapy and at home.

The point system may not be appropriate for all ages. Obviously, some teenagers may find a reward system childish. Others may not, especially if the reward provided by the parent or caregiver is age-appropriate and worthwhile. This point system can be used at the therapist's discretion and can be changed to suit the individual child's needs. Here's how it works. Each workbook activity page has a number on the bottom.

This number represents the points given to the child after completion of an activity. For example, the therapist tells the child that when he or she completes an activity page they receive the points shown on the bottom of the page. The therapist can explain that the first few pages are easier than the last pages, which will require more from the child. The therapist sets the point goal for therapy (e.g., 300 points) based on the child's own abilities.

At termination, the child and therapist count up the completed activity pages to determine the final score. Or use the worksheet provided to add up the points as therapy progresses. If the child reaches the agreed-upon point total at the end of treatment, that child will receive a prize from the therapist or child's caregiver. Some children may need to be rewarded at the midway point in therapy to keep them motivated and oriented to the tasks.

This reward system can also be used with take-home assignments. If the child brings the finished pages to the next therapy session, the points for that page are added to the child's total. This is an effective incentive for the completion of assignments between sessions. These take-home pages should not be called "homework." Instead, call them "missions" or "challenges." This will stimulate the child's interest and imagination and encourage compliance.

YOUR POINTS

Keep track of your points each week.
Add them up at the end to see if you reached your goal!

TOTAL = [   ] YEAH!

It is easier to build strong children than to repair broken men.

— Frederick Douglass

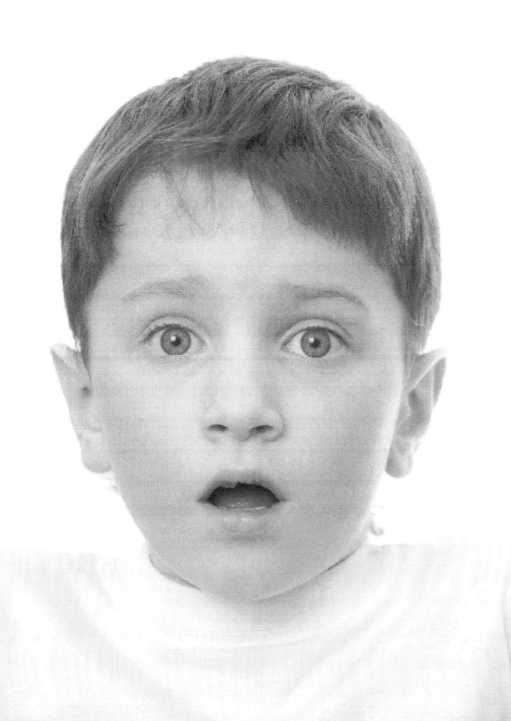

Getting to Know Me

Section Goals:

√ **Continue Assessment of Child**

√ **Build Rapport with Child**

√ **Begin Exposure of Traumatic Events**

For children who have experienced trauma, a thorough assessment is essential for proper treatment. The activities in this chapter are designed to augment your existing assessment, as well as guide treatment and help build the foundation for a good working therapeutic relationship. A detailed assessment will allow you to learn more about the child's trauma history, current symptoms and unhelpful thoughts (i.e., it was my fault that my mother beat me). Uncovering these thoughts at the beginning of therapy will give you more time to reframe or reprocess them before treatment ends.

It is very important before beginning this workbook that the child knows who you are, why you helping them and understands the goals of therapy. Below is a suggested script to use in the first session.

"I am a therapist who talks with children who have had bad things happen to them -- like the bad things that happened to you. I have heard many stories similar to yours. We'll talk about the bad things that happened to you, including the_____ (i.e., the time your uncle sexually abused you). By talking about it a lot, you will begin to feel better. Plus, I will teach you ways to feel better when you're scared, sad or angry. Ok?"

This script focuses treatment on trauma so that the child knows the purpose of therapy and that you will be talking about the "bad" experiences in the child's life. This also creates a sense of safety for the child as you are telling him or her that you will not be scared away by his or her story. I suggest using the term *bad things* as the UCLA PTSD assessment also uses these words. I have also found that it is better to say, "bad thing(s)" in the plural because often new traumas arise after the child has begun to feel more comfortable with the therapist. If the therapist assumes that only one trauma happened, the child may keep other traumatic events secret. Below is a list of the activities in this section that can facilitate the therapeutic alliance and also serve to continue the assessment of the child.

It is very important to begin the exposure process in this assessment phase and mention the traumatic experiences where appropriate in these exercises.

My Universe: This activity is helpful in determining the child's support system and who he feels close to in the family or circle of friends. I was surprised, when using this activity with a twelve-year-old boy to see that he put his abusive mother in the largest "planet" nearest to him. This was essential information as we progressed in treatment, as it helped me understand his conflicted relationship with his mother.

The Family Zoo: This projective drawing activity allows the therapist to see how the child views his family and his position or place in that family. Like "My Universe," this activity is helpful in determining which adult the child feels close to and safe enough to share his trauma story with at the end of treatment.

I'm a Superhero: The therapist invites the child to draw him or herself as a superhero, with any superhero powers they wish they had. This exercise, while clearly projective and subject to interpretation can be helpful in enabling the therapist to understand the child's thoughts about themselves. Perhaps their superpowers are abilities they wish they had at the time of the trauma (i.e., able to see future, put out fires, stop bullets, turn back time, etc.). The therapist can also ask the child what kind of "bad guys" he would catch. This sheds further light on the child's thoughts and feelings, and begins the process of rebuilding self-efficacy. If the child becomes agitated during the telling of the trauma later in treatment, the therapist can remind the child of his superhero. This may help the child regain a sense of control and reduce anxiety levels.

The Real Me: These sentence completion cards offer the therapist another avenue into the child's thought processes. This will help uncover any distorted thoughts the child has about the trauma, which then can be reprocessed in therapy. The therapist can read the sentences out loud and have the child finish them. Or the therapist can cut the sentences out and use them as part of a game. For example, when the child lands on a certain square in a board game, such as <u>Sorry</u> or <u>Candyland</u>, or picks up a certain card in a card game (e.g., <u>UNO</u>), have him pick up one of the sentences and finish it.

The exercises below are very important to re-expose the child gently to the traumatic experience. <u>What I Miss</u> and <u>What I Don't Miss</u> can be used when a loved one leaves, is sent to jail or dies traumatically. Encouraging the child to express a full range of thoughts and feelings now will make therapy easier as you approach the retelling of the traumatic event.

Time Machine: Many children harbor fantasies about what they wish had happened instead of the "bad thing" that really occurred in the past. For example: a child who was sexually abused may wish the abusing relative had been nice to her and had not been abusive. Or a child who loses a father in a traumatic boating accident may wish that the father had not gone on the trip. It is important for the child to express these fantasies if the trauma narrative is to proceed. Phrase the question to the child and incorporate her trauma. For example, "What do you wish had happened instead of your father sexually abusing you and going to jail?" *Recommended for children eleven to eighteen.*

What I Miss: Many children who have been abused by loved ones or who have lost someone to a traumatic death may harbor mixed or ambivalent feelings about that person. This exercise allows the child to express the full range of emotions about the person. For example, a child who was abused might have some positive feelings about the perpetrator who is in jail, especially if the perpetrator is a family member. They may fondly recall a time before the abuse when the perpetrator was nice and kind to them. Or a bereaved child might be sad and miss his beloved deceased uncle even though the family only expresses anger that he killed himself or died breaking the law.

What I Won't Miss: This activity follows the last one and offers the child a chance to express negative feelings about the person who died or who hurt him. For example, if a loved one dies tragically, the child may feel sad that he is gone but thankful that this person is no longer able to physically abuse him. Or if a loved one sexually abused a child, the child may miss the fun times, but not miss the abuse. This exercise allows the child to connect with the anger, fear or sadness they feel and may have a hard time expressing.

Responsibility Pie: Many children who are victims of abuse, neglect or other traumatic events feel that what happened was their fault. This exercise allows the therapist and the child to uncover the child's thoughts about their participation in the event. It is important to honor and validate the child's feelings of responsibility and also gently challenge those unhelpful thoughts.

The Hat I Wear: Children who have experienced trauma may assume a role in the family to maintain the systemic homeostasis. This could be as the "bad" kid, the "clown," the noisy one or the quiet one. Often the family places this label on the child and the child assumes the role. This label or the "hat" that has been placed on the child could hinder progress in treatment as the child feels a strong pull to wear his hat at all times. This exercise asks the child to think about what that hat means to them. Then the therapist asks the child to remove the metaphorical hat and see how he feels. This opens up the child to changes in behavior. For example: If a child comes to therapy and says he was "bad" that week, have him remove his "bad kid" hat and try on a new hat of his choosing. One therapist actually made a hat and put a label on the front to make the point. *Recommended for children eleven to eighteen.*

My Mask and Me: Another projective drawing activity demonstrates the coping mechanisms the child employs to deal with the trauma. Ideally, the child will show the therapist how they feel on the inside (i.e., small, ugly, sad, scared, angry, etc.) and how they project themselves to the outside world (i.e., strong or heroic). Or perhaps the mask and "me" are congruent. In either case, this information is helpful to understanding the child's current thoughts, feelings and behaviors. We will revisit this exercise at the end of therapy to see how they have progressed or changed in their thinking regarding their public persona or "mask." *Recommended for children eleven to eighteen.*

MY UNIVERSE

The "planets" in your universe represent people in your life.

The planets closest to you are people who care about you the most.

Write the names of these people inside the planets. Add your own planets.

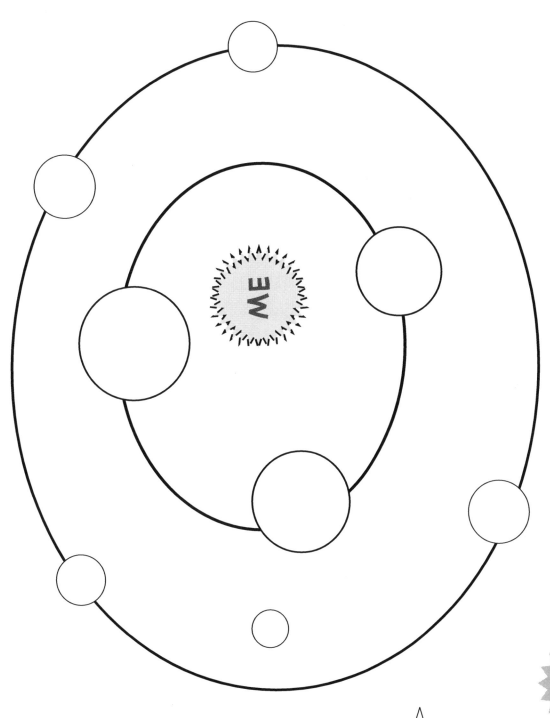

2

THE FAMILY ZOO

Pretend you and your family are animals at the zoo. Draw your different family members as animals. Which animal best describes you? What are the animals doing?

ME AS A SUPERHERO

Imagine you are a superhero. What kind of super powers would you have? What kind of bad guys would you catch? Draw yourself as this superhero. What is your superhero's name?

2

THE REAL ME

Read the sentence completions on the next pages out loud and have the child finish them. Or cut the sentences out and use them as part of a game.

For example:

When you land on a ladder in <u>Chutes and Ladders</u>, have the child pick up a sentence completion card and read it. Or... pick up a card, when:

- you slide in <u>Sorry</u> or get your piece home.
- you jump a checker in <u>Checkers</u>.
- you put a Wild Card down in <u>Uno</u>
- you put a piece on top of the tower in <u>Jenga</u>.
- you take a piece in chess.

Playing this game is worth two points in the reward system.

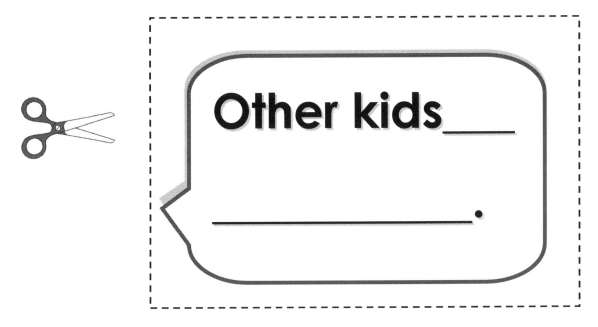

2

Other kids___

_____.

At home___

_____.

My mother__

_____.

My father___

_____.

I am sad
when_____.

I get angry
when_____.

I feel_____
_____.

Girls_____
_____.

Boys_____
_____.

I hate_____
_____.

I need_____
_____.

I wish_____
_____.

When I grow up_____.

When I was a baby_____.

My family _____.

I'd be really happy if_____.

When I get mad I_____.

If I could be an animal, I would be a _____.

If I could have three wishes, I would wish for_____.

I like my father, but _____.

I like my mother, but____.

The worst thing about me is____.

The best thing about me is____.

The worst thing I ever did was____.

I feel excited when_____.

I feel nervous when_____.

When I'm older I_____.

My family treats me like_____.

I like it when_____.

My biggest mistake was____.

My favorite place is_____.

I relax by____ _____.

I'm angry about_____.

I'm sad about _____.

I'm happy about_____.

My brother___ _____.

19

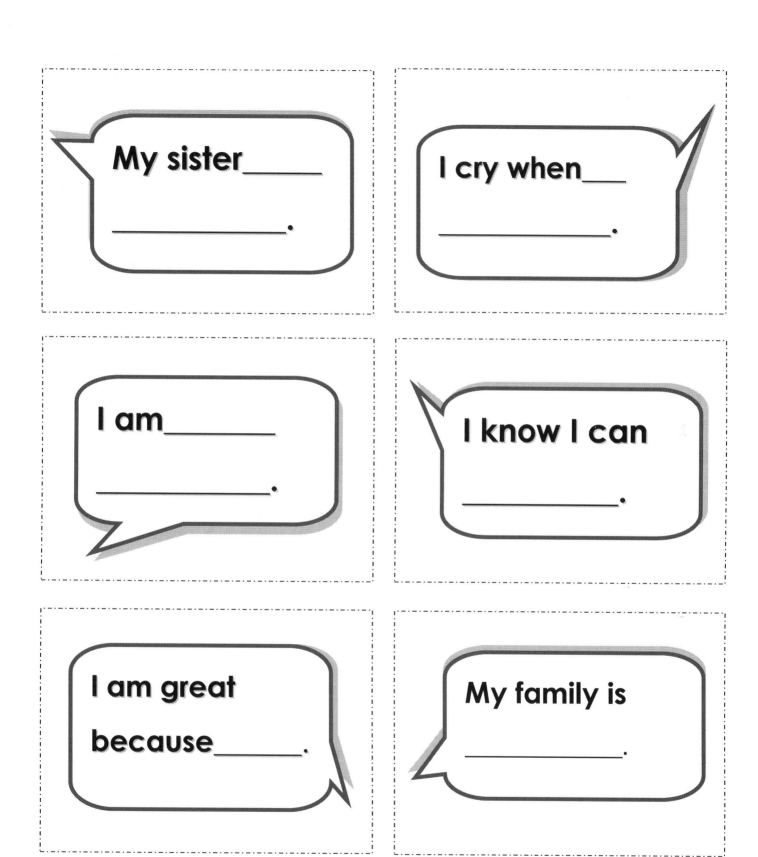

I need

_____.

I miss

_____.

My mother___

_____.

I feel unsafe

when _____.

I am_____

_____.

I wish

_____.

School

_____.

I remember

_____.

I don't want to think about _____.

My teacher

_____.

Where is my

_____?

I always think about _____.

TIME MACHINE

2

Imagine that you can go back in time and change the "bad thing(s)" that happened to you. Draw a picture showing what you wish had happened to you in the past (instead of what really did happen). We can't change the past, but sharing your true thoughts and feelings is important to feeling better.

WHAT I MISS

This is an activity if someone close to you has died or is no longer in your life. Draw a picture of the thing you will miss doing the most with that person. We can't change the past, but sharing our thoughts and feelings is important to feeling better.

WHAT I WON'T MISS

This is an exercise if someone close to you has died or is gone from your life. Sometimes we have angry or confusing feelings about the person. If you do, draw a picture (or write) some things you <u>won't miss</u> about the person. It's OK and normal to have bad feelings about this person.

RESPONSIBILITY PIE

Do you feel responsible for the bad thing that happened?

Yes ☐   No ☐

Imagine this circle is a pizza.

If you checked "yes", how much of what happened do you feel responsible for?

One piece? Three pieces? Ten pieces?

10%, 50%, 100%?

Draw the number of pieces or the percentage in the pizza pie. Discuss what makes you feel that way.

2

THE HAT I WEAR

Some kids think that their job in their family is to be bad all the time. Or sometimes kids think they have to be really responsible every day, like an adult. Other kids think that they have to be quiet and not bother anyone. Others think their job is to be the clown or the noisy one. What is the hat (or role) you wear in your family? Draw a picture of you and your hat. Can you ever take off your hat? If you can, how do you feel? Can you put on a new hat?

MY MASK AND ME

MY MASK

THE REAL ME

Sometimes we protect ourselves from others by hiding our true feelings. We don't show people how we really feel. It's as if we are wearing a mask that protects us. Draw a picture of the "mask" you wear at school or at home. Then, draw the real "you" behind the mask. How do you really feel? What do you really want to say or do?

If there must be trouble, let it be in my day, that my child may have peace.

---Thomas Paine

What is Trauma & Abuse?

Section Goals:

√ **Educate Child & Parent About Trauma & Abuse**

√ **Correct Child & Parent's Misconceptions**

√ **Normalize Child & Parent's Fears and Concerns**

√ **Begin Exposure Process**

After a thorough assessment has been completed, it is now important to educate the child and caregiver about trauma and abuse. This section offers tools for providing information on trauma and the specific forms of abuse: sexual, physical, emotional, domestic violence, etc. The proper education of trauma for the child is very important in the process of normalizing the child's feelings and correcting any misconceptions about trauma and abuse that arise. The activities included in this chapter also continue the exposure process for the child.

Equally important is educating the child's parent separately on the trauma that occurred and dispelling any erroneous beliefs the parent may harbor about the child's traumatic experience. Later, when working through the trauma narrative with the child, it will be important to meet with the parents or caregivers alone to read them their child's trauma story in pieces to slowly expose them to their child's trauma. This is imperative as they must be able to "hear" the child's trauma when you and the child share it with the parent towards the end of treatment.

 During this education phase of treatment, it is important to refer to the child's trauma directly and with the correct biological terms if sexual abuse occurred.

The following pages contain cards which can be cut out and used in a game as in the previous section. The therapist can use only the cards related to that child's particular form of abuse (e.g., sexual abuse) or can use all the cards to assess for additional abuse that may have occurred.

It is important that the therapist know the answers to the questions and feel comfortable discussing the different traumas, sexual content and human reproductive organs. If the child senses discomfort on the part of the therapist, the child will feel uncomfortable; which may hinder the progress of trauma therapy. I recommend using the National Child Traumatic Stress Network (www. nctsn.org), Trauma Focused Cognitive Behavioral Therapy (www.tfcbt.musc.edu) or Wikipedia if you are unsure of how to answer a particularly tough question. Honesty is the best approach if you are stumped. Tell the child you are not sure of the right answer but will have an answer the following week.

In addition to these cards, I recommend using the books listed on the website in Appendix B. This collection of titles, written in a kid-friendly manner, offers another tool for the therapist to educate the child on his or her specific trauma.

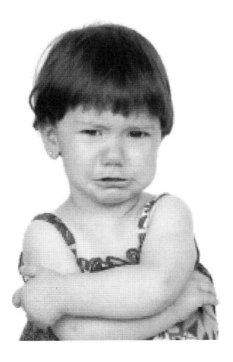

GENERAL TRAUMA

What is trauma?

Give an example.

How do some kids react to a traumatic event?

How did you react to your traumatic event?

Will you feel the bad feelings forever?

What are the physical or body feelings after trauma?

What are the thoughts some kids might have after trauma?

What do some kids do to deal with the trauma?

Why do children not like to talk about trauma?

Why do some parents not like to talk about their children's trauma?

What will we do in therapy?

Do trauma memories ever go away?

How does therapy help you with your trauma?

SEXUAL ABUSE

What is child sexual abuse?

Give an example.

What is the name doctors use for a girl's private parts?

What are some okay touches? And not okay touches?

What is the name doctors use for a boy's private parts?

Is it okay for someone to touch a child's private parts?

Whose fault is it when a child has been sexually abused? Is it ever the child's fault?

Why do people sexually abuse children?

Should you keep a secret about a not okay touch?

Does sexual abuse happen to a lot of kids? Boys and girls?

If a boy is sexually abused by a male, does that mean he will be gay when he grows up?

How does a child deal with sexual abuse?

What is sex? What is the difference between sex and sexual abuse?

DOMESTIC VIOLENCE

Is it ok for parents to fight with each other?

How should grown-ups handle problems?

Why does domestic violence happen?

Is it okay for people to get angry?

What is domestic violence?

How might a child act when domestic violence happens?

What would a child worry about if his parents fight a lot?

Whose fault is it when grown-ups fight?

Is it hard for kids to tell other people about their family's domestic violence?

What can a child do to stay safe if his or her parents fight?

What is the best way to express your feelings without hurting people?

Does domestic violence happen in other children's homes?

PHYSICAL ABUSE

When children misbehave, how should parents handle it?

Do grown-ups who hit children hate children?

What is child physical abuse?

Give an example.

Who is physically abused?
Does it happen a lot?

What should your parent have done instead of abusing you?

Whose fault is it when a child is abused?

What are ways that parents can discipline their kids in a safe way?

How does a child feel when a parent calls them names or yells at them alot?

What is the difference between spanking and physical abuse?

What does it mean to neglect a child? Does it happen a lot?

What would a child worry about if he or she was physically abused?

How can you tell a child is being physically abused?

TRAUMATIC GRIEF

Where do people go after they die?

What do you wish had happened instead?

Do people come back after they die?

What happens to a person's body when they die?

What are ways to remember people that have died?

When _____ died, I _____ and _____.

What do you wish you could do for _____?

The things I miss the most about _____ is _____.

How do people deal with the death of a loved one?

I will always remember_____.

Sometimes I worry about_____.

The bad thing I don't miss about _____ is _____.

What is the best way to know how someone is feeling?

What does love mean? How do you know if someone loves you?

Name three things you like about yourself?

I feel scared when _____.

My three wishes are:
1.
2.
3.

When I grow up_____.

Physical Abuse & DV Word Search

```
E  W  H  O  S  E  F  A  U  L  T  ?  H  I  F  B  L  W  F
C  O  N  F  U  S  E  D  C  Y  Y  N  P  D  B  U  G  T  E
S  F  O  P  ?  F  B  S  L  G  A  Y  F  ?  U  ?  H  H  S
U  Y  H  U  R  T  O  T  S  Y  D  D  E  U  G  P  O  E  B
D  B  S  R  Y  U  U  ?  ?  G  B  P  H  L  R  S  D  R  Y
I  C  A  Y  D  B  A  C  P  O  F  O  A  S  C  F  L  A  S
W  H  D  I  A  G  N  T  C  B  A  L  W  E  B  Y  A  P  E
N  O  H  E  L  P  G  U  G  U  C  I  A  D  ?  R  T  I  I
F  P  N  D  W  O  R  I  O  N  O  C  I  H  ?  B  S  S  H
I  P  S  U  D  L  Y  Y  F  T  P  E  P  D  W  I  N  T  D
E  G  F  L  W  A  G  L  Y  F  R  U  W  O  C  B  P  Y  R
G  N  ?  E  S  C  A  R  E  D  W  H  S  R  N  Y  W  L  I
L  C  S  O  H  U  C  H  I  L  D  A  B  U  S  E  D  H  Y
P  T  H  N  U  ?  G  F  E  P  T  N  F  G  A  G  L  D  N
C  N  P  Y  F  Y  R  ?  Y  U  F  G  L  I  T  I  P  G  P
```

Angry	Child Abuse	Confused
Help	Hurt	Police
Sad	Scared	Therapist
Whose Fault?		

Basic Word Search: Find as many words listed above as you can. Be sure to discuss what the words mean with your therapist and see if they relate to your own story.

Physical Abuse & DV Word Search Solution

```
E  W H O S E F A U L T ?  H I F B L W F
   C O N F U S E D        C Y Y N P D B U G  T  E
S F O P ? F B S L G A Y F ? U ? H  H  S
U Y  H U R T  O T S Y D D E U G P O  E  B
D B  S  R Y U U ? ? G B  P  H L R S D  R  Y
I C  A  Y D B  A  C P O F  O  A S C F L  A  S
W H  D  I A G  N  T C B A  L  W E B Y A  P  E
N O  H E L P  G  U G U C  I  A D ? R T  I  I
F P N D W O  R  I O N O  C  I H ? B S  S  H
I P S U D L  Y  Y F T P  E  P D W I N  T  D
E G F L W A G L Y F R U W O C B P Y R
G N ? E  S C A R E D  W H S R N Y W L I
L C S O H U  C H I L D A B U S E  D H Y
P T H N U ? G F E P T N F G A G L D N
C N P Y F Y R ? Y U F G L I T I P G P
```

Physical Abuse & DV Word Search

Words can be found across and up and down.

```
Y O U A S R E V E R Y B R A V E F O R S H A R
I N G Y I O U R S W H O S E F A U L T ? T O R
Y ! Y O B U A R E V E R Y B R A V E F O R S H
A R I N L G Y O U R S T O R Y ! Y O U A R E V
E R Y B I R A V E F O R S H A R I N G Y O U R
S T O R N S U P P O R T A L K I N G Y ! Y O U
A R E V G E N I G H T M A R E S R Y B R A V E
F P H Y S I C A L A B U S E F A M I L Y O R S
J A I L H C O N F U S E D A D D O C T O R A R
I I F N C G M O M Y F U T U R E Y H O U R S T
O N I T H R F R I G H T E N E D Y U ! Y O U A
R F G H I E O V E R Y B R A S C A R E D V E F
O U H E L P R E L A X A T I O N R T S H A R I
N L T R D O T R A U M A M Y S T O R Y G Y O U
R S I A A L A N G R Y T O R Y ! Y O U A R E V
E R N P B I B A D T H O U G H T S T R E S S Y
B R G I U C L O V E A V E F O R S H A R I N G
Y O U S S E E R S T O R Y ! Y O U A R E V E R
Y B R T E R R I B L E A V E F O R S H A R I N
G Y O U R S D O M E S T I C V I O L E N C E T
```

Angry	Bad Thoughts	Child Abuse
Confused	Dad	Doctor
Domestic Violence	Family	Fighting
Frightened	Help	Hurt
Jail	Love	Mom
My Future	My Story	Nightmares
Painful	Physical Abuse	Police
Relaxation	Sad	Scared
Siblings	Stress	Support
Talking	Terrible	Therapist
Trauma	Uncomfortable	Whose Fault?

Advanced Word Search: Find as many words listed above as you can. Be sure to discuss what the words mean with your therapist and see if they relate to your own story.

Physical Abuse & DV Word Search Solutions

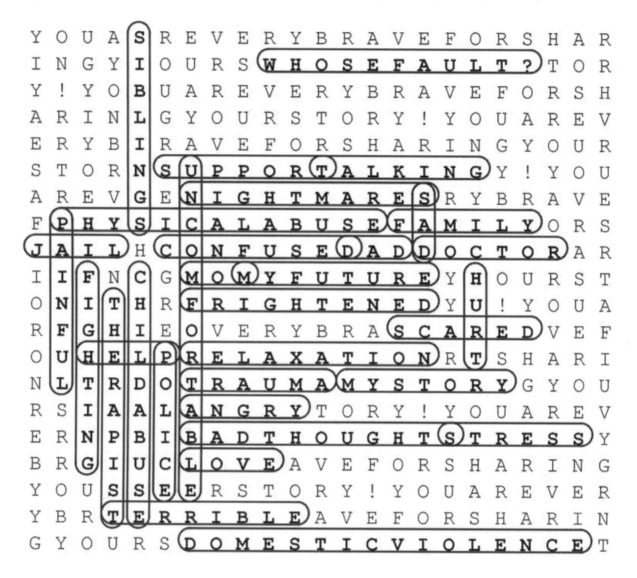

Sexual Abuse Word Search

Words can be found across and up and down.

```
W  W  Y  J  X  G  Z  X  Q  R  S  S  B  F  T  O  U  M  S
C  C  E  P  C  O  N  F  U  S  E  D  M  X  H  W  G  N  O
I  J  Y  H  S  Q  Z  X  L  A  X  F  G  X  E  Q  S  Q  K
C  T  G  G  C  U  U  P  Q  D  U  Z  R  A  R  O  B  E  K
I  G  B  G  J  T  U  R  G  V  A  G  I  N  A  E  S  H  Z
A  V  A  V  V  U  Q  I  L  Q  L  U  B  Q  P  M  C  W  Q
S  J  D  M  B  K  C  V  S  U  A  N  U  S  Y  X  A  F  P
Z  Q  T  Y  B  Y  F  A  U  B  B  O  B  V  R  L  R  F  H
E  X  O  W  Q  A  B  T  I  C  U  M  W  R  H  Y  E  F  P
B  B  U  A  A  A  P  E  N  I  S  U  T  D  Z  K  D  P  B
T  O  C  E  O  D  O  P  J  G  E  O  S  M  D  P  X  S  X
G  Y  H  H  Y  R  U  A  N  G  R  Y  H  E  L  P  O  Y  L
Q  C  I  P  O  O  T  R  R  V  C  M  Y  T  M  W  W  M  J
G  R  W  G  O  O  D  T  O  U  C  H  A  P  P  Y  D  L  Z
F  T  D  V  W  W  M  F  X  Z  I  N  N  P  D  R  R  T  A
```

Angry	Anus	Bad Touch
Confused	Good Touch	Happy
Help	Penis	Private Part
Sad	Scared	Sexual Abuse
Shy	Therapy	Vagina

 Basic Word Search: Find as many words listed above as you can. Be sure to discuss what the words mean with your therapist and see if they relate to your own story.

46

Sexual Abuse Word Search Solution

```
W  W  Y  J  X  G  Z  X  Q  R  S  S  B  F  T  O  U  M  S
C  C  E  P  C  O  N  F  U  S  E  D  M  X  H  W  G  N  O
I  J  Y  H  S  Q  Z  X  L  A  X  F  G  X  E  Q  S  Q  K
C  T  G  G  C  U  U  P  Q  D  U  Z  R  A  R  O  B  E  K
I  G  B  G  J  T  U  R  G  V  A  G  I  N  A  E  S  H  Z
A  V  A  V  V  U  Q  I  L  Q  L  U  B  Q  P  M  C  W  Q
S  J  D  M  B  K  C  V  S  U  A  N  U  S  Y  X  A  F  P
Z  Q  T  Y  B  Y  F  A  U  B  B  O  B  V  R  L  R  F  H
E  X  O  W  Q  A  B  T  I  C  U  M  W  R  H  Y  E  F  P
B  B  U  A  A  A  P  E  N  I  S  U  T  D  Z  K  D  P  B
T  O  C  E  O  D  O  P  J  G  E  O  S  M  D  P  X  S  X
G  Y  H  H  Y  R  U  A  N  G  R  Y  H  E  L  P  O  Y  L
Q  C  I  P  O  O  T  R  R  V  C  M  Y  T  M  W  W  M  J
G  R  W  G  O  O  D  T  O  U  C  H  A  P  P  Y  D  L  Z
F  T  D  V  W  W  M  F  X  Z  I  N  N  P  D  R  R  T  A
```

Sexual Abuse Word Search

Words can be found across and up and down.

```
Y O U A R E V E B R Y B R S E X A V E F O R I
S H P A V R I N A G Y O U B R E A S T S R S N
T O E R A Y ! Y D O U A S A D R E V E R Y B A
H R N A G V E F T O R C O N F U S E D S H A P
E R I I N G Y O O B A D T H O U G H T S P P
L U S U N R S J U T O R Y ! Y O U A R E V H R
P N E R A Y B A C R A V E F O R S H A S R Y O
I C N G Y O U I H C H I L D A B U S E E R S P
S O T O R T A L K I N G Y W E I R D ! X Y I R
T M W H O S E F A U L T ? P O L I C E U O C I
H F U A R E V E R S U P P O R T Y B R A A A A
E O V E F R E L A X A T I O N O R S S L T L T
R R H A R I N G Y O U R S T O R Y ! C A R A E
A T Y O M Y F U T U R E U A N G R Y A B A B T
P A A R E V E R Y B R A D O C T O R R U U U O
I B V E F O N I G H T M A R E S A R E S M S U
S L S H P R I V A T E P A R T S N A D E A E C
T E G O O D T O U C H R I N G Y U O U R S T H
O R Y ! S T R E S S Y O U A R E S V E R Y B R
A V E F O R S M Y S T O R Y H A R I N G Y O U
```

Angry	Anus	Bad Thoughts
Bad Touch	Breasts	Child Abuse
Confused	Doctor	Good Touch
Help	Inappropriate Touch	Jail
My Future	My Story	Nightmares
Penis	Physical Abuse	Police
Private Parts	Relaxation	Sad
Scared	Sex	Sexual Abuse
Stress	Support	Talking
Therapist	Trauma	Uncomfortable
Vagina	Weird	Whose Fault?

Advanced Word Search: Find as many words listed above as you can. Be sure to discuss what the words mean with your therapist and see if they relate to your own story.

Sexual Abuse Word Search Solutions

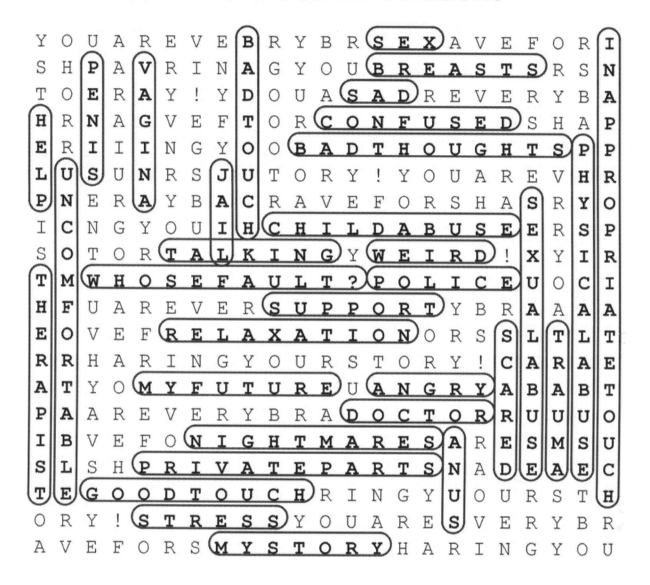

49

A lot of things you see as a child remain with you... you spend a lot of your life trying to recapture the experience.

-- Tim Burton

Managing My Emotions

Section Goals:

 Help Child Identify Their Emotions

 Provide Child Tools to Manage Their Emotions

 Normalize Uncomfortable Emotions

Children who have experienced trauma may have a hard time identifying their emotions. Some have adapted to their pain by burying their feelings, suppressing emotions deep inside. Others may act impulsively on their emotions without thought, making their life or the lives of others difficult. This section is designed to help children and teens learn to label their emotions, explore these emotions in depth and develop techniques to manage their feelings so that they do not overwhelm the child or those around them.

The following exercises encourage the child to think about how they express different feelings. Have the child fill in the sentence completions and draw pictures of themselves when they feel that emotion. Feel free to ask them for additional feeling words that further describe the five basic emotions included in this exercise. At the end of this section the child should be able to answer the following questions:

What are you feeling?   **When do you feel that feeling?**

How do others know you are feeling that emotion?

When do you feel that emotion?   **What do you do to cope?**

On a scale of 1-100, how much did (or do) you feel that emotion?

What is the best thing to do when you feel that emotion?

Scaling emotions is very important for the child and the therapist as this will be used during the retelling of the trauma to gauge how the child is managing the process. Throughout therapy, the therapist can ask the child how he is feeling (on a scale of 1 to 100). A thermometer in Appendix A can be used to help the child understand the scaling concept. If the child reports that his or her anxiety is high, the therapist can then employ relaxation techniques learned earlier to reduce these uncomfortable feelings. F   use the exercise with the outline of the body in this chapter to help the child who has a hard time identifying and expressing a particular feeling. This activity will help children better connect to the physical sensations of their emotions.

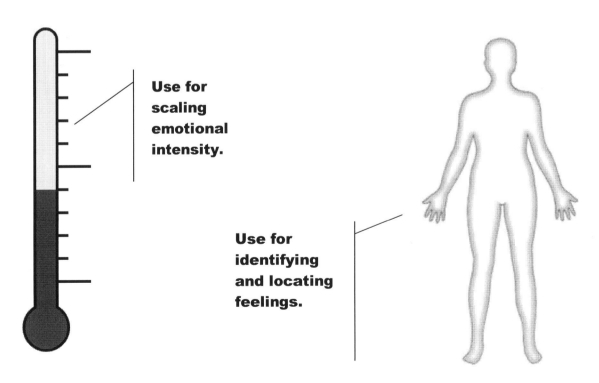

Use for scaling emotional intensity.

Use for identifying and locating feelings.

You would know I'm angry because ____.

The last time I was angry was when ____.

On a scale of 1 to 100, I was a ____ last time I was angry.

My ____ also feels angry. Who?

This is what I look like when I'm angry.

I feel angry when ____.

____ makes me really angry.

When I'm angry, I usually ____.

The best thing to do when I'm angry is ____.

What other words can you think of that describe feeling angry?

5

You would know I'm sad because I _____.

The last time I was sad was when _____.

On a scale of 1 to 100, I was a _____ last time I was sad.

My _____ also feels sad. Who?

This is what I look like when I'm sad.

I feel sad when _____.

_____ makes me really sad.

When I'm sad, I usually _____.

The best thing to do when I'm sad is _____.

What other words can you think of that describe feeling sad?

53

5

When I get scared, I usually ____.

The last time I was scared was when ____.

On a scale of 1 to 100, I was a ____ last time I was scared.

My ____ also feels scared. Who?

This is what I look like when I'm scared.

I feel scared when ____.

____ makes me really scared.

You would know I'm scared because ____.

The best thing to do when I'm scared is ____.

What other words can you think of that describe feeling scared?

5

54

When I'm happy, I usually _____.

The last time I was happy was when _____.

On a scale of 1 to 100, I was a ___ last time I was happy.

My _____ also feels _____ happy. Who?

This is what I look like when I'm happy.

I feel happy when _____.

_____ makes me really happy.

You would know I'm happy because _____.

My favorite thing to do when I'm happy is _____.

What other words can you think of that describe feeling happy?

When I'm usually ____, I ____.

The last time I was ____ was when ____.

On a scale of 1 to 100, I was a ____ last time I was ____.

My ____ also feels ____. Who?

This is what I look like when I'm ____.

I feel ____ when ____.

____ makes me ____.

You would know I'm ____ because ____.

My favorite thing to do when I'm ____ is ____.

What other words can you think of that describe feeling ____?

EMOTIONAL REACTIONS

1 Pick an emotion that you have been feeling lately.

2 If this feeling was a color, what color would it be?

3 If that feeling were a shape or object what shape or object would it be?

4 Draw that shape or object on the body in the place you feel that feeling. Use the color you picked.

5 If this feeling were a sound, what sound would it be?

6 When was the very first time you remember feeling this feeling?

7 Share that time with your therapist in detail.

8 Is there a positive feeling you want to feel more often? Draw that feeling on the body in the shape and color of your choice.

Managing Stress

Section Goals:

 Provide Tools To Manage Physical Symptoms of Stress

 Provide Tools To Manage Unhelpful Thoughts

 Continue Exposure Process

Research demonstrates that therapists can coach children on effective techniques to manage and reduce their stress levels. Through deep breathing, progressive muscle relaxation and thought-stopping, children are better able to reduce their anxiety levels and improve overall functioning.[2] The strategies and lessons in this chapter will help the therapist coach the child in using tools to manage their stress. This is important to reduce trauma symptoms and also to assist the therapist if the child becomes anxious during the retelling of the traumatic event.

---

[2] (Cohen, J. A., & Mannarino, A. P. 1998)

This chapter is broken into two sections. The first section teaches the child control of his or her physiological reactions to stress and anxiety through deep breathing, progressive muscle relaxation and visualization. The second part addresses the child's intrusive thoughts by offering techniques to stop and replace unhealthy thoughts with more pleasant helpful ones.

In addition to the stress management tools learned in this chapter, the therapist should also continue the exposure process by referring to the child's traumatic experience often. For example,"I'm going to teach you some tools to use in class when you have thoughts about the time your brother sexually abused you."

For these stress management exercises below, set the stage for the child by removing distractions from the therapy space. Explain to the child that these "tools" will help him or her relax his body and mind when stressed or preoccupied by thoughts of the trauma.

Reel Relaxation: This deep breathing exercise can be awkward for some children. The key with this technique is the complete exhalation of air from the lungs. Once the child removes all the air from the lungs, their autonomic system will kick in and force them to take a deep breath. Focus on the steady exhalation of all the air from the lungs, and the slow refilling of air into the lungs. Repeat this process ten times together with the child and you will see that both you and the child feel more relaxed. For children and teens who think this exercise silly, have them fill out the worksheet which emphasizes the importance of deep breathing for athletes and entertainers. Once the child realizes that his favorite actors or athletes use deep breathing to relax and achieve their goals, he will want to use it as well.

Robot or Noodle: Progressive muscle relaxation has been proven effective for stress reduction. To help children understand the concept of muscle relaxation, use the worksheet which asks them to draw a picture of themselves as a robot (muscles tense) and as a noodle (muscles relaxed). After they understand this concept, have the child practice moving back and forth between the two; from muscles tensed (as the robot) to muscles relaxed (as the noodle).

Stop & Go: This thought-stopping exercise is fairly simple, but requires practice to incorporate into a child's relaxation repertoire. Ask the child to name a few words that he can use to "stop" his bad memories or negative thoughts. Then, have him develop a few positive affirmations or words that he can use to replace the negative or painful thoughts.

Explain to the child that thought-stopping is great when painful or scary thoughts pop up at home or in school, but that therapy is safe place for her share those thoughts freely with the therapist.

My Peaceful Place: Ask the child to draw a picture of her "peaceful place." Have the child imagine a place where she is peaceful, happy, calm and relaxed. Once the child has created this scene on paper in detail, you can have her close her eyes and imagine this scene and her in it. Have her describe what she sees to you, what she is touching and what she is doing. Have her take a few deep breaths in this scene to reinforce the idea that this is a safe, relaxing place that she can go to in her mind when stressed. After a few minutes bring the child back and instruct her that this memory (or visualization) can be used at any time she feels anxious or scared. Have her remember this safe place when exposing the child back to her trauma. If she becomes agitated, have her close her eyes, take a few deep breaths and remember that safe place.

A Wonderful Time: Many traumatized children have difficulty remaining positive about themselves or their lives. This negative thinking can lead to depression or self-harm. To offer the child a tool to remain positive and upbeat about his life, have him draw a picture of wonderful time from his past. This could be when he achieved something great or when he enjoyed a time with friends or loved ones. Later, if the child is depressed or down, he can imagine himself back at this wonderful time to change his mood. Invite him to put this picture on his wall so that he can see it every day and remind himself of the positive aspects of his life.

My Super Safe: For particularly-anxious children or teens, use this cognitive technique at the end of each session. First, have the child draw a safe (i.e., one that holds valuables or money). Teens, if they prefer, can do this in their mind, rather than drawing it on paper. It is important that the child understand the concept that anything put inside this safe is locked away until the safe is reopened with a key. Once the child has a concrete idea of what the safe looks like, then tell her that any bad memories will be locked away in the safe at the end of each session and reopened by her (or the therapist) the next week. In this way, she feels a sense of safety that her bad memories are being kept locked up until the next week. This cognitive tool allows the child to leave her anxious thoughts behind and maintain a sense of calm and safety during the week.

REEL RELAXATION

Which of these three people use deep-breathing to relax?

1. Actress about to go onstage
2. Basketball player at free throw line
3. Golfer before a big putt
4. All of the above

Answer: All of the above.

Draw a picture above of a time when you could use deep breathing to relax. Then, practice deep breathing with your therapist. Do you feel more relaxed?

61

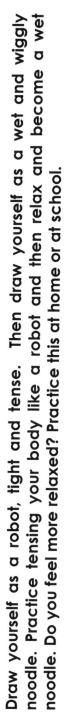

ROBOT

NOODLE

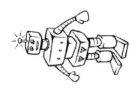

Draw yourself as a robot, tight and tense. Then draw yourself as a wet and wiggly noodle. Practice tensing your body like a robot and then relax and become a wet noodle. Do you feel more relaxed? Practice this at home or at school.

STOP & GO

Write three words can you use to stop yourself from thinking of the bad memories or uncomfortable thoughts? For example: "Stop!" Circle the one you like the best.

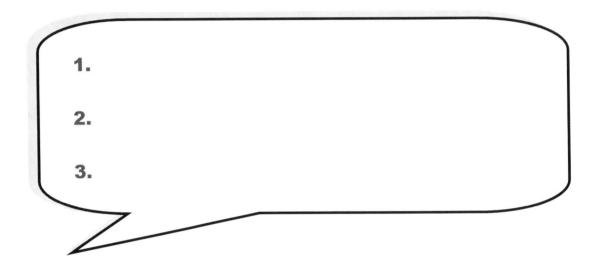

1.

2.

3.

After stopping yourself from thinking painful thoughts, what positive words or phrases can you think of to make you more relaxed or happy? Write them in the thought bubble below. Circle the one you like and will use to replace the bad memories.

1.

2.

3.

5

MY PEACEFUL PLACE ☮

5 Draw a picture of your "safe place." Imagine a place where you are safe, free and relaxed. Later, if you feel stressed, scared or anxious, you can imagine yourself back at your safe place to calm down.

A WONDERFUL TIME

5 Draw a picture of wonderful time from your past. This could be when you did something great or were enjoying time with friends or family. Later, if you feel depressed or down, you can imagine yourself back at this wonderful time to change your mood.

MY SUPER SAFE

5 Draw a picture of a safe with a lock on it. Imagine this safe holds your bad memories. Each week at the end of the session we can lock away your scary or unhelpful thoughts until we open the safe together the next week.

If there is anything that we wish to change in the child, we should first examine it and see whether it is not something that could better be changed in ourselves.

--- Carl Jung

Chapter 5

Managing Thoughts

Section Goals:

 Help Child Identify Unhelpful Thoughts

 Connect Thoughts to Feelings and Behaviors

 Change Thoughts, Feelings & Behaviors

After the child has learned to identify and control his emotions, the therapist begins to coach the child on managing his unhelpful thoughts. Unhelpful thoughts are those negative cognitions the child might have that cause stress and emotional pain. For example:

"It was my fault."   **"I'm stupid."**   **"Nobody likes me."**

Many children are not aware of their thoughts, so it is vital that the therapist help the child to explore what he was thinking at certain times. Use the thought bubble page to begin this process. Once the child is aware of his thoughts, use the cognitive triangle to explain to the child that his feelings, thoughts and behavior are all connected, and that by controlling one (e.g., thoughts), he can control the others (e.g., emotions and behavior). Be sure to explain to the child that while it's good to control his painful or unhelpful thoughts in school and at home, therapy is a safe place to share them freely.

Thought Bubbles: It is helpful for the therapist to solicit recent upsetting scenarios (not connected to the trauma) in the child's life to explain how what thoughts are, what is an unhelpful thought and how these negative unhelpful thoughts affect our feelings and behaviors. For example, a child may have had a problem at school. Ask him or her to describe the event that occurred. Then ask them to fill in the thoughts bubbles with the thoughts they had during or after the event. This exercise introduces the child to the concept of internal thoughts, which can be foreign to younger children.

My Thoughts: This is a sentence completion exercise that helps the therapist uncover unhelpful thoughts that might be affecting the child. Once these thoughts have been uncovered, the therapist can work with the child, using simple techniques to reframe and correct them. These reprocessing techniques are outlined in <u>Treating Trauma and Traumatic Grief in Children and Adolescents</u> by Anthony Mannarino, PhD, Esther Deblinger, PhD and Judith Cohen, Ph.D. They include having the child become her own best friend and offering advice to herself. Gentle questioning of the child's logic is also an excellent method for dispelling unhelpful thoughts.

The Triangle: This next exercise is designed to help further connect a child's thoughts, with her feelings and actions. Have the child or teen think of another scenario from her life that was upsetting, but not traumatic. Have her write a short sentence about what happened in the center of the triangle. Then have her write her feelings in the <u>feelings</u> part of the triangle. Second, ask her to write her <u>thoughts</u> about the event and then her <u>actions</u> or behaviors following the event. Encourage her to see how they care all connected, and that by changing one of the three (i.e., actions, feelings, or thoughts), she can change the other two for the better. Use this triangle with another example from her life. Solicit ways that they could change the scenario, by changing her thoughts, feelings, or actions. Work around the triangle so that she clearly sees the relationship between thoughts, feelings and actions and the power of changing her life by altering just one of them.

All Connected: This exercise reviews the previous cognitive processing work to help the child or teen recognize negative and unhelpful patterns of thinking or acting. Then the child is encouraged to brainstorm healthy coping mechanisms for these negative patterns.

Future Triggers: Many children who are abused may actually have contact with the perpetrator later in life, in court or elsewhere, or may be reminded of the abuse (e.g., by going into the room where the abuse occurred). Likewise, a child whose loved one has died in a tragic way may be reminded of that person's absence at future family occasions or holidays. This exercise asks the child to write out any future events that might trigger unhelpful thoughts or uncomfortable feelings. Then, for each future occurrence or event, the child develops coping tools or a coping plan for that event. For example, the child who misses his deceased mother at Christmas can tell his father how sad he is and get support from him.

THOUGHT BUBBLES

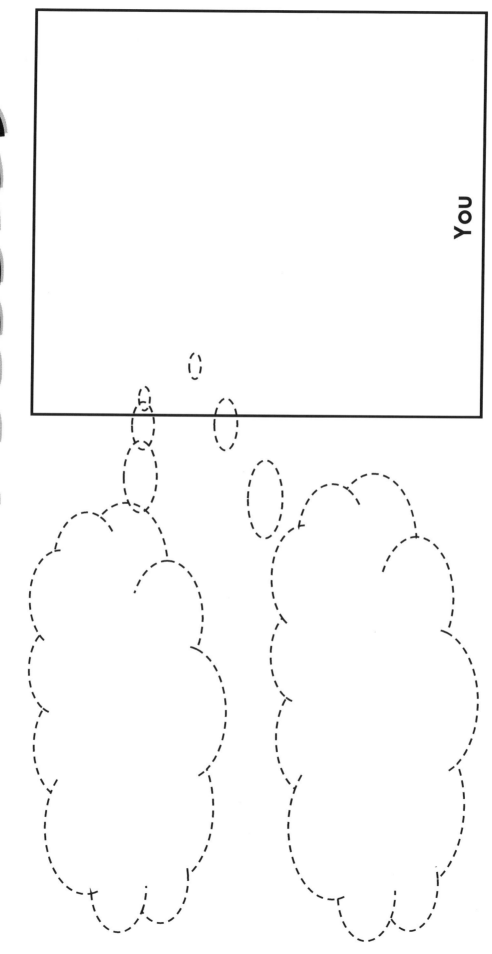

You

Think of something upsetting that happened recently. What thoughts were you <u>thinking</u> during and after it happened? Were the thoughts true and accurate? Were the thoughts helpful to you or did they make you feel worse? Draw the scene in the box and write those thoughts in the bubbles.

10

INSIDE MY HEAD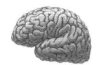

I think that what happened_____.

I think that what happened was _____ and_____.

I think I am_____.

Everybody thinks I am_____.

I think my _____ is _____.

Other kids think I _____.

My family_____.

My family thinks I _____.

I wish_____.

I also wish_____.

I miss_____.

I can change my thoughts by _____.

I can also change my thoughts by _____.

10

Finish the sentences above. Try to be as honest as you can.

MY THOUGHTS

Example: _ _ _ _ _ _ _ _ _ _

MY FEELINGS

Example: _ _ _ _ _ _ _ _ _ _

WHAT HAPPENED?

_ _ _ _ _ _ _ _ _ _

MY ACTIONS

Example: _ _ _ _ _ _ _ _ _ _

Write something bad that happened to you in the center of the triangle. Write your feelings in the feelings part of the triangle. Write your thoughts about the event and then your actions or what you did. See how they are all connected? What would happen if you changed just one side of the triangle? For example, if you just changed your thoughts? Try this with another event.

ALL CONNECTED

I feel _____ when_____ and _____. When I
(emotion)

feel this way, I usually _____ and I think _____.
(action)   (thought)

When I think _____, I sometimes feel _____ and then I
(thought)   (emotion)

_____. When I feel_____, I start to think _____.   Those
(action)   (emotion)   (thought)

thoughts make me _____. Now I know that my thoughts,
(emotion)

feelings and actions are all connected. So, to change my actions, like

_____ and _____, I can change my feelings by _____
(action)   (action)   (action)

and _____. Or I can change my feelings by thinking
(action)

_____ and _____.
(thought)   (thought)

Finish the sentences above. Try to be as honest as you can. Can you see how your thoughts, feelings and actions are all connected? And if we change one of them, the others might change too.

FUTURE TRIGGERS

Triggers

1.

2.

3.

4.

5.

6.

Coping Tools

1.

2.

3.

4.

5.

6.

Make a list of all the events in the future that may remind you of the bad things that happened. For example, if you walk by the place where the bad thing happened, or have a birthday next year and the person that is gone is not there, or the person that hurt you <u>will be</u> there. These are all "triggers." Write six triggers for you and six ways to cope with those triggers when they come up.

Each day of our lives we make deposits in the
memory banks of our children.

--- Charles R. Swindoll

Trauma Timeline

Section Goals:

 Begin Focused Exposure of Traumatic Events

 Pratice and Reinforce Relaxation Techniques

 Identify Unhelpful or Distorted Thoughts

The trauma timeline is essential in focusing the child on their traumatic experiences and creating the building blocks for their longer more detailed trauma story (often called the "trauma narrative"). This section also allows for increased exposure as the child is asked to begin to recount the events of their traumatic experience.

A. Trauma Timeline  B. Trauma Narrative

✓ **Brief Exposure**
✓ **Brief Outline**
  • *Bad Memories*
  • *Good Memories*
✓ **Therapist Shares with Parent**

✓ **Full Exposure**
✓ **Final "Book"**
✓ **Detailed Chapters**
  • **More Feelings**
  • **More Thoughts**
✓ **Child & Therapist Shares with Parent**

It is important <u>not</u> to place more emphasis on this activity than on any previous activity, as that may create anxiety on the child.

Tell the child that you are making a historical timeline of his or her life. Many children are familiar with this, as they have seen timelines in school. Make sure to inform them that this is a timeline of bad, sad or scary memories.

Begin the *Trauma Timeline* by asking the child to name the worst thing that happened in his or her life. You can also phrase this as the "scariest or saddest memory." Get enough information to fill the paragraph-sized box. Then ask for the next scariest memory. Try to fill in all five boxes so that you'll have enough content to choose from when creating chapters for the longer trauma narrative. This is especially important for children with complex trauma (e.g., foster children). Some children may have had only one very traumatic experience in their lives. If this is the case, only fill in that one experience. Be sure to ask the child how they felt during the traumatic event and include that information in the boxes.

After filling in the boxes with brief details of each traumatic experience, ask the child to rank them, with the worst one being first. This rank-ordered list will provide you with the table of contents for the trauma narrative. Share this timeline with the caregiver, without the child present, to prepare them for the child's more detailed trauma narrative. The more comfortable the caregiver is with the traumatic experiences of the child, the better the sharing of the trauma narrative by the child will be at the end of treatment. It is important though that the caregiver not discuss the details of the trauma with the child without the therapist present.

For younger children, a less complex timeline is provided. This activity simply asks them to list their traumatic experiences and draw a picture of that event. Then, in the next box, have the children draw feeling faces (e.g., sad, scared) of how they felt during the trauma. Finish this exercise by making a similar timeline with positive memories, ending the session on a positive note and helping the child realize the positive aspects of her life. This *Good Memories* timeline forms the basis for the first chapter in the trauma narrative, titled *About Me*. Below is an example of a section of the timeline. Each box should hold a paragraph's worth of information about the traumatic event and how the child felt about that experience.

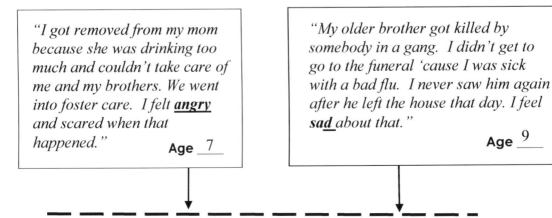

*"I got removed from my mom because she was drinking too much and couldn't take care of me and my brothers. We went into foster care. I felt **angry** and scared when that happened."* Age _7_

*"My older brother got killed by somebody in a gang. I didn't get to go to the funeral 'cause I was sick with a bad flu. I never saw him again after he left the house that day. I feel **sad** about that."* Age _9_

MY LIFE: BAD MEMORIES

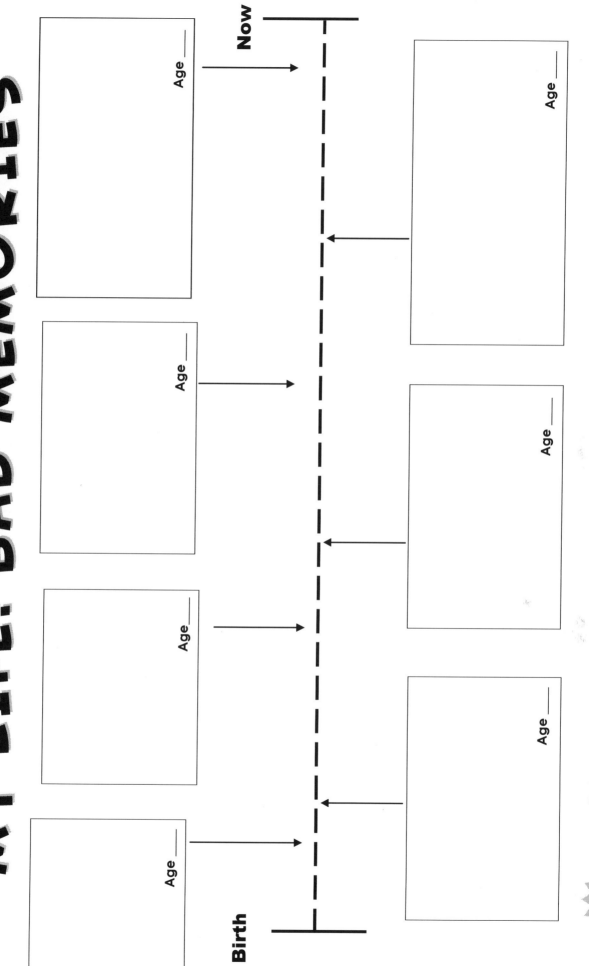

Now

Birth

Age___

Age___

Age___

Age___

Age___

Age___

Age___

Fill in the boxes with a short paragraph about what scary, sad, or bad things have happened to you. Be sure to add how you felt at that time. When you're done filling in the boxes, rank the boxes with a number, putting the worst one first.

76

MY LIFE: GOOD MEMORIES

Birth

Now

Age___

Age___

Age___

Age___

Age___

Age___

10

Fill in the boxes with the good happy memories you have had in your life. Also include how you felt at the time. It's important to realize that good things have happened to you as well.

BAD MEMORIES

USE FOR YOUNGER CHILDREN

#1 BAD, SAD OR SCARY MEMORY:

DRAW A PICTURE OF THE BAD MEMORY.

DRAW HOW YOU WERE FEELING THEN.

#2 BAD, SAD OR SCARY MEMORY:

DRAW A PICTURE OF THE BAD MEMORY.

DRAW HOW YOU WERE FEELING THEN.

#3   BAD, SAD OR SCARY MEMORY: _____

DRAW A PICTURE OF THE BAD MEMORY.

DRAW HOW YOU WERE FEELING THEN.

#4   BAD, SAD OR SCARY MEMORY: _____

DRAW A PICTURE OF THE BAD MEMORY.

DRAW HOW YOU WERE FEELING THEN.

GOOD MEMORIES

USE FOR YOUNGER CHILDREN

#1   GOOD MEMORY:

DRAW A PICTURE OF THE GOOD MEMORY.

DRAW HOW YOU WERE FEELING THEN.

#2   GOOD MEMORY:

DRAW A PICTURE OF THE GOOD MEMORY.

DRAW HOW YOU WERE FEELING THEN.

#3 GOOD MEMORY:

DRAW A PICTURE OF THE GOOD MEMORY.

DRAW HOW YOU WERE FEELING THEN.

#4 GOOD MEMORY:

DRAW A PICTURE OF THE GOOD MEMORY.

DRAW HOW YOU WERE FEELING THEN.

Creating the Trauma Narrative

Section Goals:

√ **Focus on Exposure of Traumatic Events**

√ **Practice and Reinforce Relaxation Techniques**

√ **Identify Unhelpful or Inaccurate Thoughts**

It is now time to begin the lengthier and deeper exposure work for the child. This is accomplished by creating a "book" of the child's traumatic experiences, often called the "trauma narrative." This book will then be read by the child to the caregiver (with the therapist's help) at the end of therapy.

Begin by asking the child to create a cover and title for the book. This page is provided in this section. This can be a creative artistic project for the child. Once the cover and title are created, help the child write the table of contents for his or her book. Chapter one of the table of contents is called *About Me* and is made up of positive memories from the *Good Memories* timeline (completed in the last chapter). Chapters two, three, and four are based on the three worst experiences from the *Bad Memories* timeline. Chapter five, the last chapter, is called *Me Now*, and asks the child to reflect on how he or she has changed as a result of therapy. An example of the table of contents in provided on the next page.

Example: Table of Contents

Chapter One: "About Me" = Positive memories
Chapter Two = 3rd most traumatic memory
Chapter Three = 2nd most traumatic memory
Chapter Four = Most traumatic memory
Chapter Five: "Me Now" = How I have changed through therapy

After the cover has been made and the table of contents created, the therapist interviews the child to flesh out the content for the five chapters. A rough overview for each chapter has already been created in the timeline boxes, completed previously, and now the therapist and the child expand on those memories.

Using the lined sheets of paper provided, write down the child's words verbatim. Begin with the child's positive experiences from the *Good Memories Timeline* for chapter one. The point is to have the child explain as much content as possible. This can be facilitated by simply asking "what happened next" many times throughout the retelling of the story.

Try not to ask too many clarifying questions of the child, as this may frustrate or distract him. Have them start at the beginning and simply ask: *"What happened next. OK. And then what happened?"*

Fill in the details of these good memories exactly as the child reports them to you in the lines marked "abc" on the lined sheets provided. Then reread the entire story to the child and ask her to express her feelings about those specific details. Write those feelings on the lines with the cartoon face. After finishing the feeling portion, repeat it back to her and ask her for her thoughts about the specific trauma details. Write those thoughts on the line with the thought bubble. This can take a few sessions to flesh out these three parts of the memory.

After the first chapter (*About Me*) has been done, proceed with the next chapter. This will be the third memory from the *Bad Memories Timeline* and the least traumatic. Again, interview the child to collect the exact details of the event. After capturing the event details or data, ask the child to express her feelings during each moment of the traumatic experience, and then later reread the narrative of that event, asking for her thoughts about each moment of the traumatic event. Rereading the narrative three times will increase the exposure and uncover more feelings and unhelpful or inaccurate thoughts. Use the title pages provided to separate the chapters. It is recommended that therapist make additional copies of the lined pages as the child's story may take up numerous pages.

It is important to separate out the trauma facts, the child's feelings and then her thoughts about the trauma. This is helpful for a child who has a hard time distinguishing feelings from thoughts, and also requires you to reread the narrative back to the child three times, thus increasing exposure.

After each chapter has been created, with data, feelings and thoughts, take the content you have written down on the lined pages and transfer it into the comic book template provided. This will further increase exposure and uncover more unhelpful thoughts. This also enables the child to read the book easily to the parent or caregiver at the end of therapy. While the therapist should type or write the content of the trauma narrative, exactly as transcribed, into the squares and speaking bubbles, it is important to have the child draw the pictures of the events. Leave some thought bubbles blank as well, so that the child can add more thoughts into this final version of the trauma story. Reread the comic to the child with the addition of new material, further increasing exposure.

Teenagers may want to create an art project about the trauma, writing a poem or lyrics to a song. This will facilitate greater exposure and keep the child interested in treatment. It also offers them a sense of control in the process. It might be necessary to type up the narrative for teens so that they can easily read the entire book to their caregiver or parent at the end of treatment.

Use the "worksheet" provided to continually assess the child's level of anxiety, especially during the retelling of his trauma. Use the thermometer to gauge his level of distress and check in with him periodically about his feelings. If a child is becoming anxious or distressed, use the deep breathing or progressive muscle relaxation learned earlier to help him calm down. You can also use the triangle on the worksheet to help him understand his emotional, cognitive and physical experiences and how they were all connected.

Some children will try to avoid this section. If the child is having a hard time, use the reward system to encourage him to finish the narrative. Offer him increased points if he completes a certain amount of the narrative each week.

TRAUMA NARRATIVE

_____ abc

_____ 🙁

_____ 💭
abc

_____ 🙁

_____ 💭
abc

_____ 🙁

_____ 💭
abc

_____ 🙁

_____ 💭
abc

_____ 🙁

_____ 💭
abc

_____ 🙁

_____ 💭
abc

_____ 🙁

_____ 💭
abc

_____ 🙁

_____ 💭
abc

_____ 🙁

_____ 💭
abc

_____ 🙁

_____ 💭

abc

abc

abc

abc

abc

abc

abc

abc

abc

abc

86

PHOTOCOPY IF ADDITIONAL PAGES ARE NEEDED

MY COVER

MY WORKSHEET

Q: Any unhelpful thoughts today?

Q: Any inaccurate thoughts today?

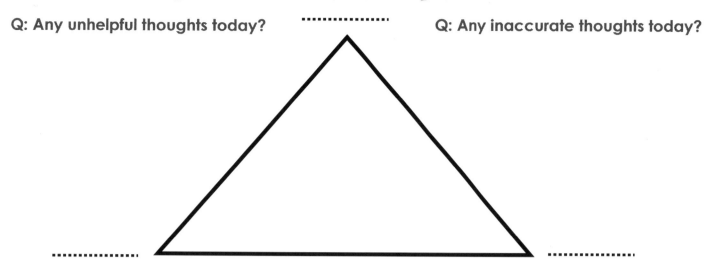

How did you feel? [0 to 100]

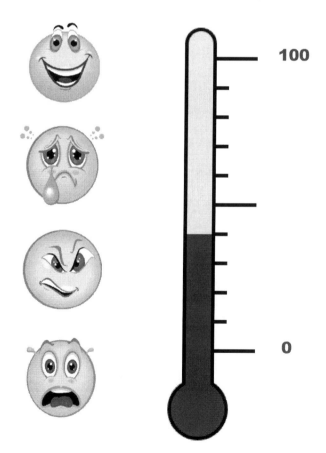

100

0

Where in your body did you feel that? Describe the color, shape and sound of that feeling.

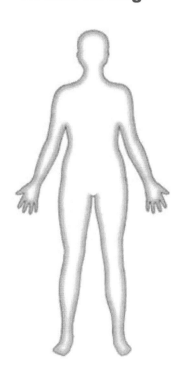

TABLE OF CONTENTS

1 **About Me**

2 **Title: "**_____**"**
    3rd Worst Memory

3 **Title: "**_____**"**
    2nd Worst Memory

4 **Title: "**_____**"**
    Worst Memory

5 **Me Now**

89

CHAPTER ONE: "ABOUT ME"

[Q: How did you feel?]

[Q: Any unhelpful thoughts?]

91

[Q: How did you feel?]   [Q: Any unhelpful thoughts?]

[Q: Could you find any unhelpful thoughts?]

93

[Q: How did you feel?]

[Q: Any unhelpful thoughts?]

94

[Q: How did you feel? 1-100]

[Q: Any unhelpful thoughts?]

96

CHAPTER TWO: _____

CHAPTER THREE: _ _ _ _ _ _ _ _ _ _

CHAPTER FOUR: _ _ _ _ _ _ _ _ _ _ _ _ _ _

Changing Unhelpful Thoughts

Section Goals:

√ **Change Distorted or Inaccurate Thoughts**

√ **Reduce Self-blame**

√ **Preparing Parent or Caregiver to Hear Narrative**

Children who have experienced trauma and abuse often have distorted or unhelpful thoughts about themselves or their responsibility for the traumatic event. Throughout therapy you have undoubtedly uncovered a number of unhelpful thoughts (e.g., "It's my fault my mother abused me because I misbehaved."). The activities in this chapter are designed to change these thoughts and replace them with healthier ones.

Unhelpful distorted thoughts differ from inaccurate thoughts. Inaccurate thoughts are factually incorrect. These thoughts are often due to the child's age or limited cognitive understanding of the events. These inaccurate thoughts can be changed often by simply educating the child to the actual events in the case.

Helping a child change unhelpful distorted thoughts takes practice, a sense of humor, as well as a directive and patient approach. Essentially, you are challenging the child's irrational beliefs. This can be accomplished with a variety of techniques, many of which are outlined on the www.tfcbt.musc.edu website under Cognitive Restructuring. Here are some of my favorite strategies:

1. **Playing Dumb.** Simply pretending to play dumb and not understanding the child's faulty logic works well. Have the child explain why they think the way they do. Ask simple inquisitive follow-up questions that serve to probe their rationale and at the same time appear to satisfy your confusion.

> **Therapist: "You think it was your fault that your brother died?"**

> **Child: "Yup."**

> **Therapist: "Hmmm. I'm confused. I thought your brother was killed in a boating accident."**

> **Child: "He was and I didn't jump in and save him."**

> **Therapist: "But aren't you like ninety pounds."**

> **Child: "Eighty."**

> **Therapist: "And wasn't your brother like one hundred and eighty pounds?"**

> **Child: "Yeah."**

> **Therapist: "So how can an eighty pound kid save someone twice his size? That doesn't make sense to me."**

> **Child: "I could have!"**

> **Therapist: "Really. Can you pick me up? I weigh one hundred eighty pounds."**

> **Child attempts to pick up therapist but is unsuccessful.**

> **Therapist: (Softly) "I'm thinking that no matter what you did you would not have been able to help him. (Child begins to cry). And I know how much you really wanted to help him, but he was just too big."**

2. **The Best Friend.** You pretend to be the child and the child becomes his own best friend. You tell the best friend your story and distorted thoughts, and then ask his advice. Most likely, the child will be more rational as the best friend and provide a more helpful realistic response to you about his own faulty thinking.

3. **The Talk Show.** Similar to the "best friend" technique, but the child hosts you on his or her talk show and provides advice to you about your story and unhelpful thinking. Again, as in the best friend technique, the child will be more apt as an advice-giver to offer more logical responses to his own unhelpful thinking.

The following activities can also be used with the above techniques to help change unhelpful thoughts into more appropriate cognitions.

Letter Exchange: Many children are confused about the traumatic events in their lives, especially if those events involved loved ones or adults whom the child once trusted. This exercise invites the child to write a letter to the person who hurt him or died tragically. Encourage the child to share his true feelings on paper with the person, knowing that this letter will never be sent. You can even tell the child that you will tear up the letter once it is written.

Once the letter is completed, ask the child to write a new letter from the perspective of the person who hurt them or died. Ask the child to imagine what the person might say back to them about their original letter. The idea behind this exercise is to have the child take on the role of the person who hurt him or died, and by doing that answer the confusing or unresolved questions about the traumatic event.

For example: A child might write a letter to an uncle who abused him, asking him why he did that to him. The child will hopefully include his feelings of anger and sadness at the uncle for hurting him. Then the child will write a response to his own letter (from the uncle) which might include expressions of love for the child and sadness, expressing regret that what he did to him was wrong.

This exercise can be very effective if done properly, and if the child understands the process. It is important to limit the coaching of the letter writing to a minimum so that the full content of the child's thoughts and feelings can be expressed. *This exercise is best suited for children ages eleven to eighteen.*

Responsibility Pie (Now): This exercise allows the child to recalibrate her feelings of guilt or sense of responsibility for the trauma that occurred. Earlier, the child may have felt more responsible for the event (e.g., "If I had walked home a different way I would not have been raped."). Through psycho-education, cognitive processing and trauma narrative exposure, the child hopefully is gaining a better understanding of her limited role in the traumatic event. This exercise is presented twice to show the child how far she has come in reshaping her beliefs about the trauma in her life. If the child still feels largely responsible for the trauma, it might be useful to spend more time on cognitive reprocessing and investigating the family dynamics that are maintaining the homeostasis of her beliefs. *This exercise is best suited for children ages eleven to eighteen.*

Heavy Blocks: This activity also asks the child to discuss her goals with the therapist and the "blocks" that are weighing her down or preventing her from reaching her full potential. Draw four rectangle blocks above the small man on the page with pencil. (Using a pencil is important as you will erase each block once you and the child have come up with a solution for that problem). For example: The child tells you she wants to have more friends. But the 'block" you draw above the man is that she is shy and ashamed about the trauma. Together, therapist and child decide that the child is to talk with one other child a day at school. Once agreed upon, child can erase the block and feel freer to reach that goal.

Fly-Away: In this exercise, children let go of unhelpful thoughts or unpleasant memories, writing them in the balloons that are flying away. The thoughts and memories they want to keep are written in the balloons tied to the line.

The Name Game: Children who have lost a loved one to a traumatic death need an opportunity to reflect on that person in a positive light, as a way to finalize their grief work. After the child has offered any ambivalent or negative feelings about the person in an earlier activity ("What I Won't Miss"), the child can now remember positive attributes of the person without the complication of hidden feelings. This activity asks the child to write the person's name in the boxes on the left and then use each letter in the name to begin a sentence describing something positive about the person.

Unhelpful Thought Cartoons: This activity allows the child to review all the unhelpful and distorted thoughts uncovered in therapy and write them into the cartoon boxes provided. This is very effective in summarizing the cognitive work done in therapy to date.

My Mask & Me II: This activity repeats the first one ("My Mask & Me") where the child was asked to draw a picture of the mask they wear to hide their true feelings. The objective of having the child repeat the activity is to gain greater congruence between inner and outer expression of feelings.

How Have You Changed: This important exercise asks the child how he has changed a result of the hard work done in therapy. This page can be included as the last chapter in the trauma narrative.

"Me Now" Chapter Title Page: This is the final chapter title page of the trauma narrative. The child draws a picture of himself as he is now, at the close of therapy. Ideally, this chapter title and picture reflects a more positive outlook for the child.

IMPORTANT

After these above cognitive reprocessing exercises, put the trauma narrative together into book form, with the covers, table of contents, chapter titles and any other information the child wants to include. Once this is completed, have the child read the book to you cover to cover, preparing for the reading of the book to their parent or caregiver. This reading of the trauma narrative (now in book form) by the child to the caregiver or parent is very important for the child to feel safe, accepted and loved.

Before the child reads the trauma book to the parent, it is essential that the therapist meet with the parent alone to prepare them to hear the traumatic story. Read the child's book to the parent so the parent is not surprised by what the child has written. The parent may become emotional. Process these emotions with the parent, but explain that it is important the parent NOT become overly emotional when the child reads the story to them, as this may be upsetting to the child and could derail the process. Many caregivers need to be exposed to the content a few times for them to be able to "hear" the narrative without becoming too upset.

Caregivers also need to be coached on "how" to hear the trauma book. Anxious caregivers may need to do deep breathing while the child reads the narrative to them. Reinforce the idea that the child only needs them to listen. Encourage the caregiver to simply thank the child for sharing the story, offer any feelings in the form of I-statements, and then give the child a hug. Too much exposition from the parent may detract from the child's sense of mastery of the trauma narrative.

LETTER EXCHANGE

Dear

_____

_____

_____

_____

_____

_____

_____

_____

_____

_____

_____

_____

_____

_____

_____

_____

_____

_____

_____

_____

 15

Write a letter to the person that hurt you or is now dead. This letter will not be sent! Put all your honest feelings in this letter and also feel free to ask any questions you may have about what happened to you and why.

Dear

15

Write a letter FROM the person that hurt you or is now gone. Pretend you are him or her and you are writing a letter in response to your own letter. What feelings would you express? What answers would you have to the questions you asked in the first letter?

RESPONSIBILITY PIE: NOW

Do you feel responsible for the bad thing that happened?

Yes ☐   No ☐

If you checked "yes", how much of what happened do you feel responsible for now?

One piece? Three pieces? Ten pieces?

10%, 50%, 100%?

Draw the number of pieces or the percentage in the pizza pie. Discuss what makes you feel that way.

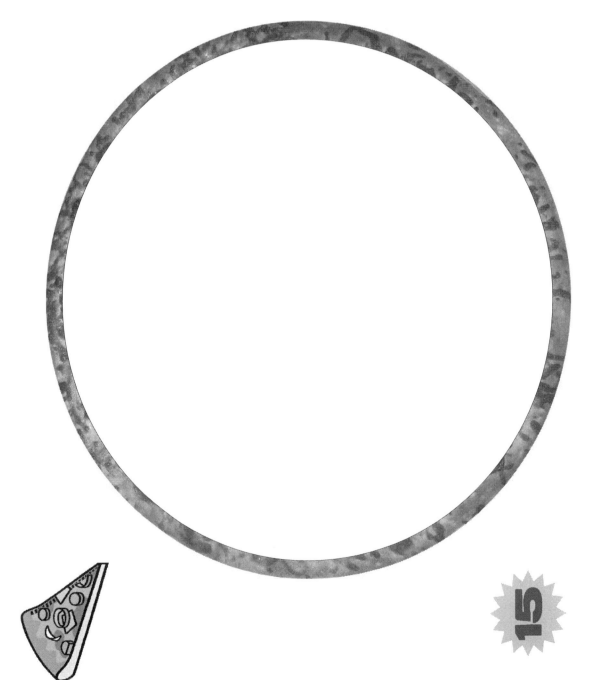

15

HEAVY BLOCKS

I DON'T KNOW WHAT TO SAY ABOUT WHAT HAPPENDED

I FEEL ANGRY ALL THE TIME

I'M TOO SHY.

NO FRIENDS

15

Use a <u>pencil</u> to draw four big rectangle blocks on top of each other directly over the man above. See example to the right. Inside each block write something that is making you mad or sad or keeping you from your goals. With your therapist, try to find solutions to each block. After you find a solution to that block, erase it to lighten the load. Now do that with the other three blocks. Does the pressure feel less now?

FLY-AWAY

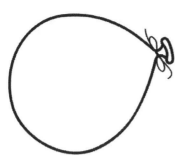

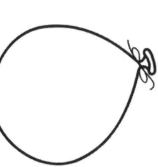

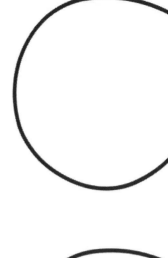
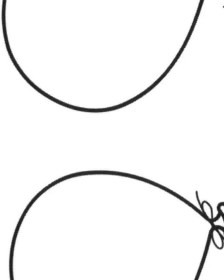
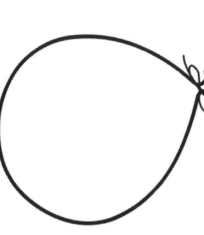
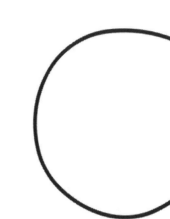

Write the memories and thoughts you want to <u>let go of</u> in the balloons in the air (i.e., "it was my fault"). Write the happy thoughts and memories you want to <u>keep</u> inside the balloons tied down (i.e., "therapy helped me").

NAME GAME

☐ _____

☐ _____

☐ _____

☐ _____

☐ _____

☐ _____

☐ _____

☐ _____

Example:
Terrific Dad Who Always Smiled
Invited me to baseball games
Made me laugh alot

Use this exercise if someone you loved died or is now gone. Write the letters of their first name vertically down the left side of the page. Then, using the letters of his or her name, make sentences that help you remember the good things about that person. An example is above.

Unhelpful Thought

Fill in the blanks and draw in the pictures to show how therapy has helped you.

I used to think that_____ _____and____ _____.

But now I know that_____ _____ _____.

15

Helpful Thought

111

I used to think that_____ and _____.

But now I know that_____ _____.

Unhelpful Thought

Helpful Thought

Unhelpful Thought

I used to think that_____ and
_____.

But now I know
that_____
_____.

Helpful Thought

15

MY MASK AND ME II

```
┌─────────────────────────┐
│                         │
│                         │
│                         │
│                         │
│                         │
│                         │
│                         │
└─────────────────────────┘
```

ME

```
┌ ─ · ─ · ─ · ─ · ─ · ─ · ┐
·                         ·
│                         │
·                         ·
│                         │
·                         ·
│                         │
└ ─ · ─ · ─ · ─ · ─ · ─ · ┘
```

MY MASK

15 Draw a picture of the "mask" you hide behind to protect you. Then, draw the real "you" behind the mask. Did your mask change from the first time that you did this exercise?

HOW HAVE YOU CHANGED?

THEN

NOW

Have you changed since coming to therapy? Write how you were before you started therapy and how you are now. Do you notice a difference?

FINAL CHAPTER: ME NOW

America's future will be determined by the home and the school. The child becomes largely what she is taught; hence we must watch what we teach, and how we live.

--- Jane Addams

Safety Planning

Section Goals:

√ **Develop Safety Goals for Future**

√ **Celebrate Child's Completion of Therapy**

This chapter focuses on developing healthy skills to protect the child from abuse or violence in the future. The child is asked to think about future scenarios in which she might find herself and how she would handle himself. Use the contract provided as a way to discuss the safety measures the child can use in the future. Have him sign the contract and read it to his parent or caregiver so that both caregiver and child are in agreement on measures to take to prevent the abuse or trauma from occurring again.

At the conclusion of therapy it is important to celebrate the child's success with a graduation ceremony and party. Present the child with the certificate provided as evidence of his achievement in learning new tools to manage his thoughts and feelings and in sharing his traumatic experience with you. This ceremony is key to the child's sense of accomplishment and positive feelings towards therapy, which are essential if he needs to return to therapy later on in life.

MY CONTRACT

I agree to _____

when _____

_____ and/or _____

happens so that I feel safe and keep myself from

being hurt again. It is important for me to

_____ in the future so that

_____ and _____

doesn't happen again.   I will also talk to

_____ when I feel scared or

unsafe in the future.

Signed_____ Date _____
Signed_____ Date _____

20

In the future, when I feel mad or sad or scared, I can talk to these people that <u>support</u> me.

Write their names in the blocks below.

Draw a picture of you on the top block.

20

CERTIFICATE OF COMPLETION

This certificate certifies

Name: _____

Has successfully completed therapy!

GREAT JOB!

Therapist: _____

HOW DO YOU FEEL NOW?

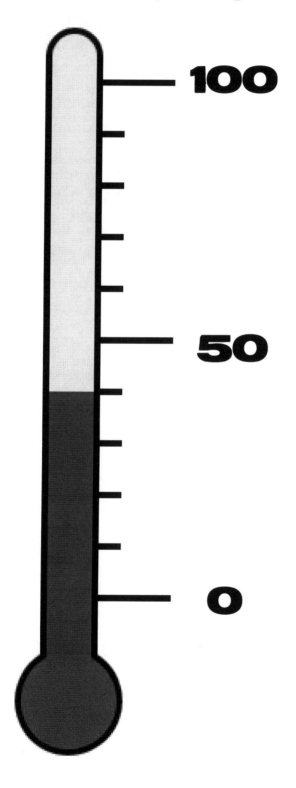

References

Cohen, J. A., & Mannarino, A. P. (1998). Interventions for sexually abused children: Initial treatment findings. *Child Maltreatment, 3*(1), 17-26.

Cohen, J. A., Mannarino, A. P., & Knudsen, K. (2004). Treating childhood traumatic grief: A pilot study. *Journal of the American Academy of Child & Adolescent Psychiatry, 43*, 1225-1233.

George Sachs, Psy.D. is a licensed clinical psychologist and trauma specialist. He is a graduate of Emory University and the Illinois School of Professional Psychology. Dr. Sachs completed his pre-doctoral training at Mt. Sinai and Cook County Hospitals in Chicago, working with abused and neglected children. He then finished his internship and post-doctoral residency at the Children's Institute in Los Angeles. Dr. Sachs provided supervision and training in TFCBT (Trauma-Focused Cognitive Behavioral Therapy) to clinicians in the Los Angeles area.

Currently, Dr. Sachs lives and works in New York City. He is the founder of the Sachs Center, a private practice in Manhattan, focusing on ADD/ADHD and High Functioning Autism in children, teens and adults. Dr. Sachs uses a holistic approach, going beyond labels to take a person-centered view of treatment.

Dr. Sachs is available for trainings, consultations, speaking engagements or interviews. Please direct all correspondences and inquiries to george.sachs@sachscenter.com or call him directly at 646-418-5035.

" Dr. Sachs was instrumental in starting the TFCBT program in an area of South Central Los Angeles, where it was needed most. He was able to adapt the protocol to cases far more complex than the normative sample. His workbook reflects an evolution in the field and the indelible mark he left upon the Childrens Institute, Inc. site here in Watts. "

--- Dr. Robert Strong, Staff Psychologist, Trauma Team Leader, Childrens Institute, Watts Office, Los Angeles, California

FREE DIGITAL DOWNLOAD

If you would like a free download of this book, facilitating easier use of printing and photocopying, go to http://www.trauma-workbook.com

1. Add the digital download of the book to the cart
2. Type the word *friend* in the discount area. That will reduce the cost of the book to zero.
3. Then checkout normally and you will receive a link for the free digital download of this book.

71466006R00075

Made in the USA
Lexington, KY
20 November 2017